THE EEL LADDER

Nancy Jane Bullis

watershedBooks

Photographs and design by Nancy Jane Bullis

Allan Briesmaster, Editor
A.F. Moritz, General Editor
Mary Ellen Csamer, Editorial Review

Titles typeset in DomBold;
Text typeset in ComicSans
Printed in Canada by The Coach House Printing Co., Toronto

watershedBooks
71 Fermanagh Avenue
Toronto, Ontario,
Canada   M6R 1M1

Canadian Cataloguing in Publication Data

Bullis, Nancy Jane, 1956 -
     THE EEL LADDER

Poems
ISBN 1-894205-10-3

I. Title

PS8553.U477E34 1999   C811'.54 C99-930877-7
PR9199.3.B782E34 1999

Like a seismograph, the poetry of Nancy Jane Bullis intimately registers the shocks and aftershocks of contemporary living. Bullis amplifies and plays us back the tragicomic voices buried in society's wreckage: voices of the casualties, stunned survivors and those pushed over the edge.

> "I wish my life wasn't so pathetic but I know there are no surf boards here and the life boat's out there saving someone else."

In the end, what unifies this multitude of sonic "ladders" is no easy harmony, but a compelling chord of recognition and concern.

"Sometimes I wonder how all those who do not write, compose or paint...can manage to escape the madness which is inherent in the human situation."

Graham Greene

In memory of
everyone I've known who died too young

It's been way too many
to comprehend

And it's been going on since
I was just a kid full of song about some guy and his rowboat

Table of Contents

Part 1

Table of Contents, continued

Part 2

Part 3

Part 1

Condiments

There's salt and pepper in the backyard
but at first I didn't notice
enough for the barbecue
enough for Aunt May's wedding day
the second time around

Must grow on oak trees just like love
they said during dinner
I was late and eating appetizers

I was too late for the main course
too late for the meat
but there's salt and pepper in the backyard
pass the shakers, I said, it's so nice here
and someone gave me cheese

The Sun in June

I want to be clean like the sun in June
on your back
warm and what you've waited for all week to bask
like a Grecian Urn to turn
like an unspoiled egg to bake like a
cake in an earthquake unharmed and
the moment of wonder when all about
is an insurer's nightmare where to dream
is to be your reality and all about is your
favourite food untainted by pollution or solutions for a
better something that to
strive is to
attain and to attain is to
have without the want of something more or
someone else

I guess I feel the same but wish I didn't somehow wish
I knew when to stop like a gambler who understands the
symptoms and overcomes it all and stops with the jackpot
that the dealer knows isn't mine if I keep playing and
I wonder what it means to be content without losing it first
without saying if only I knew I had it all before I bet it
all on that guru guy

I want to be clean like the sun in June but
it doesn't feel the same if it lasts all year and
maybe it's more romantic to lose than to drudge it out
like scraping the windshield in winter because you know there's
a car in there somewhere and maybe what we are is like a bag
of milk at the grocery store and other
things so mundane that our dreams go beyond
each other into other places with foreign faces and
lives we've never met that make us feel like
we are growing when it is harder to
feel the depth of grey

And maybe I am just an old lazy girl who looks the same and
talks the same as yesterday and not like the sun in June that
seems to understand the beauty of absence and that
returning is sometimes better than something new and
when it comes it's time to celebrate time to let it
happen because we know the passing of a
month and maybe if I was like the
sun in June we could have a
celebration or if not a
celebration at least a moment on the deck when you
turn over like an animal to have your belly scratched

Eating Breakfast

There's no such thing as a rich artist, said Dad
while I was eating Cap'N Crunch and Cheerios
if you become a poet, he said,
you'll never own a car without rust

I know some poets who are so good, I said,
they own brand new Chevrolets and some country

Yes, he said, but they're not rich from their art
the only time true art costs money is when
the artist's dead

Teenage Wednesday

Carol
stands on the corner
rolls her own one-handed
waves at Sue and Larry as they honk by
in their fluorescent green-bottomed Dodge Charger
Lancaster Perch or Bust reads the bumper

Carol, hair hanging
holds her rollie to the sun
pulls the tip only slightly till it's bang-on straight
pops it in her mouth
lights it
sulphur in the air
stares at the water puddle beside the curb

She turned 17 on Saturday

Frankie scuffles up with a mickey of scotch stocked safely
under his arm like a lady's handbag full of I.D. and memories
tells Carol stories of when he was a kid
yep, me and Louis had a belching contest
Louis won when he belched out the first
four bars of O Canada, heh, heh, heh

Carol asks Frankie what'll happen when the puddle dries up
and Frankie says, it'll rain, kid
Carol sinks back in the weathered bench that reads
It's the Real Thing and
rolls her own one-handed

Dogs

My sister makes tomato soup from beef broth, wants to see if the vegetarians notice. She knows that the likes of me were brought up in the Waspaterian way and won't ask the question, What's in the soup anyway?

Use what you've got, I heard growing up, eat your beans, drink your milk, wait one hour after eating before you play baseball.

I have learned how to eat several small meals a day. It is not good to bloat the stomach, makes it want more.

Push to the limits of who you are, said my elders, reach for the moon, if you get two steps outside your back door you're doing well.

My will took me farther than my backyard and the city I grew up in, but I'm not so sure why I'm standing here. I walk through the grocery store, worry about the price of starch foods, and whether I can afford extras.

These are the questions my elders asked when I would throw butterscotch toffees in the grocery cart. Is that on the Canada Food Guide? they'd say, Can you live without toffees?

Yes, and other things people I meet at reunions talk about: mortgages, car insurance and saving for a rainy day.

I like to walk in the drizzle, just enough to get my nose wet. My peer is a dog who is happy when his master feeds him and takes him to the vet when he has ticks. The difference is in how we communicate our ailments. He scratches his ear until it bleeds. I recede into what is accepted. His master sees the signs, who is my master?

You are the master of your destiny, said a psychic, who told me other things about me that I never knew like the time I was a Yankee nurse who fell in love with a Confederate soldier.

There is still a war somewhere, the possibility of romance.

Tetherball

He wanted to be like us, that kid
to be badder than bad, smarter than smart
not him, the honest type, called me his friend
said I was nice to him but my peers told me to stop
so we made a deal, him and me, that he did what I said

We fixed his belt loop and swung him
the centre of our attention, he laughed at first
but like most times I've trusted too much
we pushed too hard, too fast
his head struck against the pole
we watched it, all of us
I think of it now when I hear
the clanging of an empty flag pole

When I used to think about things that are over
my sister would always say, you can't change what is, forget it
which is what she did about most things that
would happen to me
I'm not so sure it's the same with things that
had happened to her
like the time I bought lye soap to wash my clothes
you smell of poverty, she said

Like the time, him and me, we had dinner
it was the empty dessert plate we savoured
pointing to the place where the sugar shortbread sat
he pressed his finger to the white china saying
that was the best
a recognition that exists only between us

I've lost touch with those I played tetherball with
but him and me, we've stayed friends for many reasons
guilt is one of them

Daffodils

I heard that a housewife from Georgia found happiness
and my nephew says that he feels happiness every time
he looks at the daffodils

A friend said that he knows happiness during sex
and a guy on the bus said that happiness comes from
repentance

A woman in the park said that happiness comes from knowing
pain and when the hurt isn't here,
the pain goes away once in a while

My nephew promised to show me the daffodils whenever
I want to see them
his flowers don't know the passing of rain
they're protected by the leaves of his scrapbook

Chloe

Everything's white chocolate wallpaper covered with peonies
hot pink like my heart...ripples in the paper
have to brush the wrinkles out
to the bottom
to my ankles
to my feet
cut off my feet...

> Move your feet
> I cannot see because your feet are so big
> they're bigger than your head...
> Cut off your head
> but not mine, no, take it off
> take it all off and we
> will make love
> on the church steps at four in the morning
> our sex will ooze on the wallpaper

> Hello!

They're here, I knew they would come
the soldiers in their dirty white shoes

> Take off your dirty white shoes!

But they never do and they won't say the word penis out loud
to me

> Sit here, Chloe
> put your arm there,
> Chloe

Hell, I'm older than them who think I'm stupid
besides I have to find my man
they think I made him up

He wants to buy me Sulfur Mountain
our sex will make avalanches
the mountain goats will have to move in with the soldiers
but he doesn't know I'm here

I've seen the game plan of egg salad sandwiches, drugs,
no sugar
it's all that girl's fault, that daughter of mine
oh, she's not, but she's such a waif I had to make her mine...

> Take off your feet!
> But you never do
> I have to find my banner that says
> Take off your feet!

I live in a conspiracy but I'm not too tired to fight
I will find my man
we will make love in the best place without feet
and that waif of mine can have all my shoes

Always looking for the perfect pump, she says
hell, she doesn't know the meaning of shoes
because there isn't one!

I am tired now, I have to go to sleep
my man will be here when I wake up
I sent him a message with my eyes...

Talk about Town

I remember the time we went fishing. He played guitar and I listened to his voice all afternoon. The fish didn't bite but I had some money saved from my last job so we went down to the chicken place where he told me that I was wasting my time with him.

I just wanted to drop some acid but he said he would never be the one to introduce me. He protected me, told me to go away once in awhile, guess he was dealing or something. I never really knew.

I liked to feed him and bed him and keep the camp going, even when I got that new job and I had to leave the camp. I said I'd be back and I was but the camp was gone when I got there and I thought he left me because...well, I didn't know why.

When I went into town no one talked to me for a long time, three weeks I guess, and then someone told me where he was. I never told anybody about anything, not that I ever knew and he never acted like I did when I went to see him at the courthouse but other folk talked. You know, like, what was I doing with him, and then I guess they decided that I talked. I never thought he thought I did, even when I saw him after he got out of jail but he didn't say much, like it changed him, and all I remember him telling me was to stay outside.

I saw him a few months after that, arm around some blonde in line at the disco, that's how long ago it's been, and then I heard he was working as a janitor down the street from where I was living at the time. People said he didn't want anything to do with me. I don't know if it's true, but that was the talk about town.

Pigeons

Fairy tales always told me, you just know when you find Mr. Right, and my mother used to say, look for ambition in a man but learn how to pay the bills anyway, just in case. Joshua used to say, I love you just because, and I thought that he would die if I married him. So I never did even though I knew that he was right for me. He found a woman who didn't think he was destined to an early death. He's still alive, and so is she. Marriage didn't kill either of them, 10 years now. I feed the pigeons and scratch my head. They do too, their own heads, not mine. I would never get that close to a bird unless I was going to eat it.

Dealing with the Facts

Upside down on a fence post
an empty cup
rattles in the wind

There's no steadying emotion until
the wind dies down

Laundry

This woman on the subway said that
she can tell when she's living with a
Canadian because she always finds
the flag in the washing machine

Up your Canadian flag, she said,
I don't have enough bounce to
make it cling free

Texture

Life is like corduroy
I wish it was felt

When I Think of You

I feel like a glove turned inside out

It is a nice glove

Either way
there are always preferences for
the other side

I was a Samurai Once

A guru told me
at a friend of a friend's house party

It's in your blood, he said
the killer instinct
why don't you carry a sword anymore?

I don't miss it, I said
thinking about the spider I squashed
in the shower that morning
it didn't even rain

Nostalgia

When you look in magazines you see models
in designer clothes from when you were a teen
that are not the clothes you wear in photo albums
and your kids say, Mom, you looked so stupid

Eggs

Standing on the driveway chewing bubblegum, poodle Muffy hugs her side. She wants to paint the dog's hair pink like bubblegum, eye shadow. She hears her mother say, Mona, I don't know why you put that pink cream on your eyes, makes you look like there's something wrong with you.

She wonders if there is, and why her best friend Sandra told her mother, that's Mona's mother's sister, that secret about Mona and what's-his-name. Mona told Sandra not to tell anyone or she would die. Sandra asks Mona, why didn't Teddy call you back like he said he would? And Mona says, he will.

Her neighbour Cam, playing road hockey with what's-his-name, strikes her in the knee with a filthy ratty tennis ball. She bends over to pick it up beside her pink toe nails and royal blue rubber thongs she bought on sale at Woolco Monday. Her back hurts. She thinks she's getting fat. The snap in her jeans screws her belly button.

Before she knows it her thongs are gone for slippers fuzzy that don't make loud click click sounds like those white ones she wore for her honeymoon. Sandra said they'd look sexy with that fancy nightie Teddy gave Mona the Christmas before they got married in a double ceremony with Sandra and Cam. Even then, Mona said she was fat, but that was a lie compared to now.

She looks at Teddy across the table, sipping coffee, reading paper in that blue checkered flannel shirt he likes to wear when he goes on hikes with Poncho. German Shepherds aren't cute like poodles, he says, but they're better protection for the kids, and for you.

Mona cracks the last egg against the counter, writes eggs on the grocery list.

Her mother always told her to play the field when she was young. She did, she said, with what's-his-name. She knows his name even though she told Teddy she can't remember. She doesn't want to hurt Teddy like Sandra hurt Cam when she ran off with everyone-knows-who from Oregon. Her mother talks about it still, with Mona but not with her sister 'cause they'd end up fighting, and they want to be good neighbours, so they don't mention Sandra, or the baby, who isn't really a baby anymore, 16 now, the same age as Mona's girl.

Mona pours more coffee for Teddy. He asks her if he should buy more stock in Canadian Tire or try Bell for a change.

Mona looks out the window, watches her daughter standing on the driveway, chewing bubblegum. She nods to her husband and says, yes, dear, you did call, even though it took you a while.

That's Why Mick Jagger is My Hero

My mission in life used to be
to track down a baby blue Volkswagen Beetle with
a sunroof on the street somewhere parked with the metre on
and the owner gone just so I could leave a note for the owner
that says
I love your baby blue Volkswagen Beetle with a sunroof

Ever since I heard Mick Jagger is in town
I now look for a Rolling Stone
Mick Jagger to be precise just so I can
walk up to him and say
Cheers Mate
that's all and walk away
that's all and say to myself I met my only hero who is still
my hero from childhood
the only one who did not fall down somehow from
some fatal flaw that's all and
Maggie says, Why is he your hero anyway?

Because, I say, he never made excuses for who he was
never acted like who he wasn't but
I can't say that being a chameleon in high school just so
I could fit in with
the smart crowd
the in crowd
the drop-out crowd
never did fit in with the jock crowd
don't know why

My whole life would be different if I did fit in with the jock
crowd maybe but probably not
just like my whole life won't change if I do find
a Rolling Stone, Mick Jagger to be precise, or I do track down
a baby blue Volkswagen Beetle with a sunroof

These little missions in life are what I do and
what I talk about when I sit at the bar watching
the baseball game
the hockey game
the latest scandal unfold of some
celebrity somewhere and
everybody wondering what went wrong
spouting out drunken words of insight about how
they would have done it different if
they had all that money
it's just a bunch of crap
most stuff said in bars is just a bunch of crap
even though sometimes someone falls in love
not that it happens every day or happens to me

Well it happened once
twice I guess
three times
maybe more I don't know
but I hate it when
some stranger sits down and says so
what do you do and I say hi
how do you do and he says no
what
do
you
do?

Well, I say
I look for a Rolling Stone
Mick Jagger to be precise
sitting in a baby blue Volkswagen Beetle with a sunroof
on the street somewhere parked with the metre on and the
owner gone
just so I can leave a note for the owner that says
I love your Volkswagen Beetle with a sunroof just so
I can walk up to Mick and say
Cheers Mate
that's all and walk away
that's all
and say to myself I met my only hero who is still my hero from
childhood the only one who did not fall down somehow from
some fatal flaw
that's all
not much I guess but
it's my life and
it makes me happy and
that's why Mick Jagger is my hero

Back Dive

I stand on the subway platform with my heels over the ledge, pretend it is summer camp.

I am 12 again, 96 pounds, competing for the back diving championship. I look over, see Nick the lifeguard who reminds me to breathe deep, hold my head high. I arch my back, can't wait till I have breasts, don't care if I win another championship. Nick says that I don't see the big picture but I do one night when I am supposed to be at vespers. Sneak away to smoke cigarettes underneath the awning by his bedroom where I hear him talking. Have to look, then I can't stop watching him and Trudy, the girl who's all dots and circles. The guys love her and I am just another diver, as shapely as a knife. I sit at the table of champions, stand up when my name is called. Nick is in the audience with his arm around Trudy. He gives me a wink and a thumbs up like it is enough.

My life has been a series of competitions. I fall in love with my mentors who are always in love with someone else. It's what I do. My toes grasp the subway platform ledge. I prepare for the cleanest back dive I have ever made, but decide to forget it. Too easy to outspeed the train, but this guy runs up, grabs me anyway, just to be sure, he says. It's not Nick. I ask him if he's married and he says, yes, and then he says, I know you, aren't you... Yeah, yeah, I say, give me your number and I'll tell your wife you done good.

Directions

I want to be the director, I say, and make him put his hands on her breasts. She looks at me like, what are you doing, me with your boyfriend in front of you? It's a moment when no one's sure how much I know, and I say, you want to be in pictures don't you? And she says, yes, but not this way. And what way do you want, I say, fiction?

We don't stay friends after that. I didn't have any film in the camera anyway. He was only my boyfriend sort of. It wasn't like when I was younger and believed that the merchant fairy would bring me a rich man. He was just another guy without a bank account. I don't even think we said good-bye.

She used to be a friend of mine, a dancer who dresses like Marilyn Monroe. She used to say that I've got to expose myself, and I'd say, yeah right, and she'd say, no, not that way, you've got to go where the millionaires are. And I'd say, where's that, on a yacht off Crete? She'd say that I'm not a realist and I'd say, okay, get me a gig at Bunny's Burlesque, and she'd say, that's not the place for you. Surprise! She always had advice for me. I wanted to do the same for her, but she'd always say, who invited you?

Who invited me? I did. Cut.

One of Those Days

It's just one of those lousy days when the snow is mounting and your best friend doesn't want to talk to you and your boss is having one of those days too and you wish you had called in sick but there's no one at home to take care of you and your nose is running but you're out of kleenex and toilet paper and paper towels and napkins and no you don't want to use the sanitary ones but what choice do you have when you hear your cat crying because you think he's got frostbite and a collector calls about a bill you forgot to pay and then this old boyfriend from hell who you haven't heard from in years decides to look you up and you just want to escape to your favourite soap opera but it's been preempted for some late breaking news-cast about some politician who you never even voted for and all you want to do is go home to Mommy and cuddle in her skirts and drink her hot chocolate but you know you're too old for that even though it would feel so good to hear the words everything will be okay from someone you actually believe in which in turn would give you this compelling urge to hug her back and thank her for having you

Corn Dogs

We can go to the moon
we can go to the planet of Mars
but he can't pick up the telephone

I guess he's too busy flying his machine or
eating corn dogs

He told me once that he loved me because
I like corn dogs

Eating corn dogs is what I do when the world is mucked in
black leather, t-shirts, motorbikes and rock bands

I feel so at home when someone calls out,
Hey you, pretty missy, you can win a big prize, and
the band sings, Are you rich enough?

When he said he loved me I just laughed
feeling stupid is what bosses, enemies and kids are for
not lovers
but I have this alien bitch that comes out sometimes of
the knee bone, the ankle bone, the chest bone

I want to barefoot on the beach with him

Maybe I'm a seagull
maybe I'm a scavenger
looking for men
I'm always looking for men
but I say no because of him unless
I think they're gay, it's okay I think
if I think they're gay
I have been wrong

I don't know why he doesn't call
I flip the Tarot through my fingers
Tarot tells me that he thinks I live in
Never Never Land that I
bit his hand that I'm
just a female Peter Pan
so he takes his plane up in the air, the air
the sky gets darker way up there

He wants to travel into space
walk on the moon in running shoes

He pulls the throttle to the floor
nosedives to the ground, the ground
where it's all brown
the ground gets bigger, biggest, best
but he knows
he knows the distance and
he takes it

Spaghetti

The airplane you were on
left on Tuesday
I was making spaghetti

It wasn't very good
but neither was your flight
or so I saw on television
you were one of those hostages
they showed bandaged under the
green light

You always wanted to travel
I wanted to cook

Petunias

He bends down to kiss one
he saw his neighbour do it once
petals on his lips soft

Must be a pleasant thing to do
like holding babies and cooing them
imagining their futures

People have babies all the time he heard
not always by accident
or for some pre-conceived notion

Something else
from inside and higher
than the genitals moves them

Petunias are not the same
he kisses one then kisses others

Corkscrew

Have you got one? he said, and grabbed my hand

No, I said, have you? and grabbed his hand

If I had one, he said, would I ask you? and swung my hand
behind his back

If you had one, I said, and swung his hand behind my back,
you might want two

And with his foot, he caught my foot,
and what, he said, would I do with two?

That's up to you, I said, and caught his foot,
you might sell two and buy one new

And what, he said, should I do with you?

You can't, I said, sell me too

No, he said, 'cause you can't move

Without you, I said

Without you, he said

He said, I'm twisting you

I said, I'm twisting you

He said, the wine is due

I said, what shall we do?

The wine, he said, we'll break in two

Like me and you, I said

I'll drink to you, he said

And I, I said, shall drink to you

And if I said I love you...

would you say, I love you too?

I don't mean it in the big ell way or
the carnal sense, but the other kind

I would bake a chicken, slice a lime
like I always do, but it would taste
so much different

Rapids

I couldn't help him that day in the rapids with his canoe
my own boat was full of water and I was afraid of drowning

He cried for help from someone as weak as him
saw me as the strong one and blamed me

Like him, I met the shore alone
watched him turn his back to me and disappear into the trees

I was going to sell my canoe or stop boating but that wouldn't
make us friends again and those boats got us home
I'll remember that

I'll remember him sometimes, probably wish I could send him
a postcard, yet he'd see it as a victory
I can't pretend I meant to let him down

I want to make the hollowness go away
deny the very shape that keeps canoes above the water line

It's time for me to smooth the roughness of the wood
challenge those rapids without him

Linseed Oil

It's been
seventeen moves in fifteen years
few consistencies except maybe a lot of time
spent buying things and throwing them out
something I had to go through to find out
what's important
a knife, a fork and my old school desk
from days of ink wells

One of my first acquisitions and I still
haven't refinished it
simple, solid oak
it would be easy to do
a little linseed oil and a few Saturday afternoons

It's amazing what time can do when you
polish the same spot
that's what he was trying to tell me eight years ago

Delayed reaction
there's no refund for time spent on
foolhardy purposes
no other way it could be
it was necessary to the process
something I never put any value in
process
always wanting the latest colour
the newest song
I thought it uninteresting to watch something grow

~

I had my first fire in the fireplace last night
stoking the embers I ran out of wood
I could only poke for so long before
all I had left were dinosaurs
extinction hasn't stopped scientists from searching
for what went wrong
I've been blaming myself for my own
conservation

~

The pictures aren't on the walls yet
each time the choice changes except for a few
the dog
the boy with the wine and
Churchill

Picked Winnie up for the price of the frame
I was into eyebrows at the time
the essence of the man
understanding failure
didn't capture me until after my days dating
in a cartoon land

~

Books are easy to unpack
not much thought to know where they go except if it's
alphabetical
chronological or
by genre

My dream was to live in a science fiction theme park
being an alien from another planet I was
always planning my escape to the time of teleports or
the place John Lennon wrote about

Imagination isn't always a good thing, he'd say, asking
When's dinner?
Only mortals eat, I'd say,
a fundamental difference in our lifestyles

I have since learned how to cook simple meals
what it's like to count vitamins
I didn't know how satisfying limitations could be

~

I like to eat goat, something I didn't have the patience for as
a child always lifting the lid
Is it done yet?
How long will it take?
Can I go now?

As an adult I leave when I please
not always understanding that
time is the greatest reasoner
not to say that I left too soon or
I shouldn't have at all or it took too long to recover

Acceptance begins with yielding to what can't be
forgotten about myself just like that old school desk

On Saturday I am going shopping for a little linseed oil
and a chamois

Part 2

THE EEL LADDER

I

I am eating a hot dog in my tree. I like eating hot dogs in my tree. I do not like eating hamburgers. I think that people who eat hot dogs will save the world. I think that I will be great when I grow up not only because I eat hot dogs but because I have the insight to avert hamburgers...

II

I am at my friend's house. She is learning to sew. Her sister is learning to sew. They are making a shift dress. The pattern is designed with acorns in tawny brown, black and green. The acorns on the front of the dress are upside down. My friend is crying. I think the dress is totally original. I think my friend is totally original. My mother and I make a shift dress. I want to lay the pattern upside down. My mother tells me that everyone will laugh at me because I dress like a clown. I lay the pattern upside down. I think my friend's dress and my dress are different. Her dress has upside down acorns. My dress has upside down tea kettles. My friend and I are different. We go to different schools because we are different. She is French and Catholic. I am English and Protestant. I wear my dress to school. I miss my friend...

III

Gordon beats me up during recess. Michael squishes worms in my hair. Morris follows me home from school and swears at me. My teacher says that I should be happy that so many boys like me...

IV

I am at the piano. My mother wants me to have culture. My music teacher dresses like a butterfly and dances when I get the metre right. She wants me to be Miss Canada, but if I want to be Miss Canada I must practice four hours a day and I cannot ski or play baseball. I like to practice four hours a day. I like to ski and play baseball. I do not like the idea of parading on national television in a bathing suit and high heels...

V

I am at summer camp. It is run by a church. We have vespers at dusk. I would rather listen to bullfrogs than hymns so I sit by the lake and smoke cigarettes. I think that Export "A" are better than DuMaurier. During the day I sing O Canada when the councillor raises the flag and I go to swim class because I like talking to the lifeguard. His name is Nick. Nick teaches me how to dive. I like to jackknife. At first I am afraid that I will smash my head against the board. Nick tells me that I will never realize my dreams if I am afraid. I think that fear is bad...

I am in the summer camp mess hall. We are having macaroni and cheese. I like macaroni and cheese. Nick likes macaroni and cheese. Nick never misses lunch, except this time. After lunch, the councillors tell us to look for Nick and I find him by the lake face down in a canoe. It is the first time I see a dead person. It is the first person I know to commit suicide. My friend says that suicide is a sin against God and that I should love God. I think that God is dead but I do not want to kill myself. I sit in my tree and wait for God, just in case...

VI

I am in Washington, D.C. camping with my family. The grounds are surrounded by barbed wire fences and Rotweillers. I am eating liver. I do not like eating liver. I shove as much liver in my mouth as I can and go to the washroom. I think that there are hidden cameras in the washroom filming me as I throw the liver into the toilet. I think that they, whoever they are, will tell on me. I hear voices that tell me to kill my master. I tell my mother about the voices. I do not tell her about the liver. She tells me that my master would never let me kill my master. I tell her that I know that Nick is not my master. My mother tells me that it is not my fault that Nick is dead. I did not want Nick to die. I do not want to kill my master. I do not know if I am afraid of the voices that tell me to kill my master or of the voices that tell me that Nick blames me for his death. I tell myself to not be afraid...

VII

I am at the dam with my father. We are comparing the different water levels on each side of the dam. My father tells me how the turbines under the dam churn the water into electricity, that the turbines churn the wildlife too. He tells me how the turbines cut the eels in half and that he thinks that it is wrong to kill the eels. He shows me the ladder that he built for them so that they can climb the dam above the turbines. I ask my father how the eels know to use the ladder and my father says that they just know...

VIII

I am at university. I do not like being at university. I change my registration to part-time. I like rock and roll and the blues. I like to bartend in a rock and roll blues bar. I am not a good waitress. I almost lose my job and one of the house musicians asks the boss to give me another chance. The house musician gives me J.D. Salinger novels. I thank him but I do not sleep with him because I am living with a guru who drinks Blue and has a beautiful dog. I tell my parents that I have my own room. They buy me a bed that folds into a chair. It is a brown corduroy chair. I like brown corduroy. I want to buy brown corduroy jeans before I go to see Jethro Tull. We listen to Jethro Tull a lot. We have a lot a parties at our house and listen to Jethro Tull. I get tired of coming home and finding a party in my house. I leave the guru but I miss the beautiful dog. I visit the beautiful dog and the guru strikes me. I am surprised when he smashes my head against the floor. I am afraid that my parents will find me dead and that my mother will notice that I did not wash my hair. I tell myself to not be afraid...

IX

I am at my graduation. My friend does not come to my graduation. My parents buy me a black velvet suit. It is a beautiful black velvet suit. I wear it when I bartend. The guru is barred while I am working and I am happy. I like my customers, especially the biker guys. They tip me well. I do not like the girl who is a transvestite. She tells me that I won't serve her because she is different. I tell her that it is not because she is different. It is because she is drunk. She gets mad at me and I serve her anyway. My boss finds her passed out on the sidewalk outside the bar. I only gave her one beer. My boss says that it doesn't matter. It is still my fault. I want to say I am sorry to the transvestite girl but she is slumped in the backseat of a cab going south...

I am in a car with my boss's coke dealer. I like my boss's coke dealer. She is a topless masseuse. She hates her customers. She hates my boss. She knows when he is dry. She stands on his desk with the bag in the air and makes him tell her that she is God...

I am sad when the bar loses its liquor license. I think that I will always be a bartender and never a writer. I know that I will miss the people, especially the house musician who gave me J.D. Salinger novels. He tells me that we won't lose touch. I like making love to the house musician who gave me J.D. Salinger novels. When I am in the hospital, the doctor tells me that he thinks the house musician who gave me J.D. Salinger novels gave me something else...

X

I am making a fluorescent green Audrey Hepburn-type dress. I am sad that my relationship with the house musician who gave me J.D. Salinger novels is over. I am tired of wearing black leather, spandex and spike heels. I think that it is time for something different, a little fluorescent green Audrey Hepburn-type dress. I do not look like Audrey Hepburn in my Audrey Hepburn-type dress and I think I want to kill myself but I do not like the options. I tell myself that I will never kill myself. I sit at the dam in my fluorescent green Audrey Hepburn-type dress and watch the eels climb the ladder...

XI

I am at medical school. I am surprised that I got into medical school. I do not like being at medical school. I do not like some of the boys. I do not like some of the stories that they tell about me. I do not like the story about me being the best sex they ever had. I do not like some of the girls. I do not like some of the stories that they tell about me. I do not like the story about me being the stupidest person they ever met. I wonder if I really am the stupidest person they ever met. I am afraid that I am too stupid to pass medical school. I tell myself to not be afraid...

XII

I am in my office. The patient in front of me has just been told that he is terminally ill. I tell him about his options. He tells me that he wants me to do more than just kill the pain. I like being a doctor. I do not like playing God...

XIII

I am in my office eating a chicken shwarma sandwich. The phone rings. It is my mother. She tells me that my father had a massive cardiac arrest. I am surprised that my father is dead. I miss him more than I thought I would. I think about hanging out with my father and watching the eels climb the ladder...

XIV

I am at the bar watching O.J. Simpson going south in his White Ford Bronco on the L.A. Freeway. The TV reporter says that O.J. Simpson is suicidal. I do not think that O.J. Simpson is suicidal. I do not think that I am suicidal. I do not care what happens to O.J. Simpson. I do not care what happens to me...

XV

I am in my doctor's office. My doctor tells me that I am clini-
cally depressed with suicidal tendencies. He wants to put me
on Prozac and send me to a mental health professional. I do
not want to take Prozac. I do not want to talk to a mental
health professional. I want my doctor to talk to me. I like it
when my doctor talks to me. He tells me what it's like to be a
World Series Champion. He tells me what it's like to be
anonymous in medical school. He tells me about how he likes to
watch birds. We talk about Canadian Geese and how they
never fly in a perfect V formation. We talk about the leader
at the front of the V, that he isn't really leading, that he is
just flying there. When he gets lost, he doesn't quit, he
changes direction. Sometimes some of the birds fly with him
and sometimes they don't. Sometimes he flies alone for awhile.
My doctor says that there are times in his life when he feels
like he is at the front of the V and times in his life when he is
not. He says that it is difficult to be at the front of the V
when he is lost but that it is better to know that he is lost
than to be following somebody else who is lost. I tell him that
I know that I am lost. He tells me that I am on his 24-hour
crisis list...

XVI

I am in my doctor's office. I feel like I am always in my doctor's office. My doctor tells me that it is because I am in his office at least once a week and that I call him on the telephone 24 hours a day. I tell him that I am not afraid of death but that I will never kill myself. I tell him that I have done extensive research on suicide and that I am in a low-risk gender and age group. I tell him that I have inventoried suicide victims in literature, that I have read real life accounts of near-death experiences from attempted suicide victims, and that I have read the philosophy on euthanasia from the Hemlock Society. I show him reports on suicide that I carry in my briefcase. I have newspaper articles on suicide from all over the world. My doctor tells me that I am still on his 24-hour crisis list...

XVII

I am at the dam watching the eels climb the ladder. I know
that the eels do not know that my father is dead. I know that
the eels do not care that my father is dead as long as they can
use the ladder. I know that I will always care that my father
is dead and that I should use the ladder that he built for me...

XVIII

I am eating a hot dog in my tree. I like eating hot dogs in my tree. I think that I was wrong about thinking that I would be great when I grew up because I eat hot dogs. I still do not know if I am wrong about thinking that God is dead. I wonder if God is dead like Nick and my father. I do not know what it is like to be dead and I wonder what it will be like to die. I wonder if my life will flash before my eyes like I heard it will and if I have remembered all the relevant points that will flash before my eyes. I wonder if I have forgotten any of the salient points and if I will be surprised by what I have not remembered. I am not afraid of death but I am afraid that I will not die in peace. I wonder more than anything else if I will die in peace. I tell myself to not be afraid...

XIX

I am eating a hot dog in my tree. I like eating hot dogs in my tree. I do not like eating hot dogs without relish. I am out of relish. I think that it is time to get some more...

Part 3

Shadows

I used to think it was so mundane to make shadows
a puppet show for those who do not like to sew and yet
playing is so important in a child's life
a developing life

I want to be a developing life till the day I die

And how I like to play with light and shadows and the
filaments of death that filter
through the room
through my life
through my relationships
to you

I am mystified by our bodies
lying side by side

I am mystified by our minds
lying side by side
and I wonder what would happen
if we joined them in intimacy

I like to think about your shadow and mine
what they look like together to others but
nobody knows when perception is everything

I've wished upon a satellite
when I thought it was a star

The shadow doesn't know
how long it will be my shadow

Shadows
I used to think they were so mundane

Popsicles

The world is full of popsicles
molded and folded into forms to fit a flavour

Name a flavour of allegiance
you're one of them like me

It's better tasting the world of popsicles
as a popsicle besides
where would we be without flavours?

Where would we be without sticks?

There are those
who sandwich themselves into corners without sticks
and those who dance to their own drumsticks in their own
freezers
without associating themselves with you and me

Don't let them thaw you out

It's tough in here
wishing we were lemon when what we are is orange
rubbing paper with high society creamsicles
bubble headed shortcakes
macho Mr. Bigs and unforgiving Crispy Crunch

You are what I need in this world full of wood and ice

Heroes and Gloves

Reading the voices on pages before me
I feel the white paper
flat with smooth edges
longer than I can see or will ever breathe

They were my heroes in high school
who will inherit my son
who will inherit my baseball glove

It is a good glove of Cadillac calibre
said the salesman
it will last longer than you

I wonder why the glove people made it that way
I wonder who makes the heroes

Trains

I miss hanging out at the trains
how my first love took the train
with me to an Irish pub
wrote little love notes on the shamrocks

My mother thought we were going to elope
we didn't know how to elope
we didn't know how to sign the hotel register
but there we were just trying to do that
Mr. and Mrs. Jones, we heard a song called
Mr. and Mrs. Jones or something like that

My mother said
he was no good for me
twenty years later she just says
I was too young

I don't mention men to her anymore because
I don't know if I'll find the one
I want to marry
but I do know that my soul mate is Nostradamus

We talk through a student at UCLA and Lake says
you guys should get it together

Nosti's so right about World War III
where we're going and why we're going there
and I think that there's more than one anti-Christ

Nosti, I want to hold you in the middle of the night
when the bombs go down
Rwanda's screaming so loud
Oklahoma's mourning its babies and
I'm so scared

Politicians, politicians don't understand
they don't understand that the boundaries have been broken
we're not talking country loyalty here
we're talking the world
we're talking the spirit of the world

Nosti, I'm in the universe now and there's no rules yet
everybody's going for control while
the cyberwarriors are fingering their friends
making connections

I want to hear more about the
spirits and the gods
the war is brewing
the Nazis are back

I learned how to fight
I leaned how to take all those people on with their
so called brassadorio
I can stand my own against brains
but I can't stand my own against bombs
I can't stand my own against
monsters who prey on the children
they could have been the ones to challenge
the corporate claws
the hatemongers' bytes
the powers that be
in heaven and in hell
forever and ever
but they won't get the chance
they're all victims in some sort of power struggle
we're all victim to it...

Nosti, it's funny how you have come from
the other side to the cyberspace that we
meet in a place without bones
but I still want to take the train

Trains
how I miss hanging out at the trains
how I want to take the train with you
to my mother's house
I hope Lake can make it
I'll get us some tickets for Mr. and Mrs. Jones
it's a good song, Nosti, Mr. and Mrs. Jones or
something like that

Nosti, have you ever seen a train?

Leather Lattice

I miss you and your leather lattice
how we used to hang ourselves from hooks on your
leather lattice
pretend we were dead
leftovers from a queen's war without ceremony without
sense of funeral just hanging
in mid-air without audience until our flesh hardens
falls into the earth
our bones ornaments on your leather lattice

My fantasy was to die with you but
you lost interest in me and the game of death or so you said
took your leather lattice with you when you
moved away from me
said you burned it but I knew you didn't do that knew you
wouldn't do that because a leather lattice costs too much

When your brother called
he said he found you hanging in mid-air
on a hot Thursday in July on your leather lattice
all by yourself

I thought you were gaming me
I wanted to say
I wanted your bones
I wanted your leather lattice
but your brother said he burned you
he burned your leather lattice and I wanted to say
you burned me, it's not the same but
you burned me just the same

Fish and Chips

I wish Joe would give us dinner money instead of this garbage every night. Here, eat mine. I don't like fish and chips. Susan used to say, eat your fish and chips. Jackie used to say, read the paper. I always wondered where the paper had been. What the stories were in the paper. I wonder if your paper has the story about the murder of that girl. She was so young. Sixteen. She was stalked in broad daylight for about two miles. She was in grade 11 and very popular. She wanted to study business administration at a nearby university. She hoped to specialize in the textile trade. She knew her killer. She didn't try to run away but was followed for quite a distance. She let him walk beside her. There were footsteps in the snow. She was wearing size seven Kauffman's with a 3/4 inch heel. They were black leather. The killer was wearing size 10 Kodiaks. They were brown leather, well beige actually. You should eat your fish and chips. They'll get cold. There was a struggle in the bush off the main highway. She was strangled. Her books were strewn beside the road. She was going to do her math homework for the test the next day. Her killer was a dropout. He completed grade eight and, at the time, was looking for a job. He is in the restaurant business. His last job was as a dishwasher at a fish and chip store. He was fired for being late too many times. The victim had a younger sister. The killer was an only child. His parents were killed in a car accident when he was four. He lived with his father's brother and his second wife. They had no children. They raised bloodhounds. At the time of the murder, there were 12 bloodhounds living in the house. The killer's guardians and the victim's parents played Bridge every other Thursday. The two men grew up together. The funeral was held at the W&S Funeral Home. All donations were made to the Heart Fund. Her name was Susan. Her younger sister's name is Jackie. Susan said I was retarded and wouldn't know how to read the paper. Jackie would always say, Stewart, read the paper for Susan, and I never could. Hey, where are you going? Eat your fish and chips.

Icebergs

When it's cold outside
it's easy to talk without passion
nine-tenths below the surface

When it's hot inside
it's easy to think that icebergs melt

Break the surface and the
temperature
drops
like the odds

Rock

When he skips a rock
I think about being in the air and
how a good rock fights five or six times to stay there

The last splash never seems to be what it is for observers
I think it must be different for the rock

I never promised anything but to be on the shore
when he got there

Interactive Imagination

My beach blanket radio's still humming while
my slow mode modem doesn't have a podium no more
and my cellular's on celluloid beside my vintage Kodak

Mr. Bob from the film lab's been calling me
to pick up my shots from 1990-something
I know he wants his money honey
it's only fare, a little bit to build the empire
but I can spin my head-on existence into my
serial port and
download my image into
digital video audio and
make a virtual instant postcard
without a handshake

I wish you were here
Mr. Bob
and then I wouldn't have to go
all the way there
and spend all that time
in underground capsules built for the space world
where everything is physical and
strangers have voices that
I can't delete to my trash bin
without the fear
that someone
is going to push me
over the edge

I want you
I want you
to be my interactive imagination

I love the sound of trees meeting a June breeze and
blowing grass between my teeth
the confidence of youth and
the anxiety of desperately attempting to keep a radio station
in tune when I am driving out of range

I love the smell of lilacs and blueberries and
men when they touch my skin

It feels so nice to be at home
after all those years of watching others
from the local beer on tap and
reading magazines
feeling the boredom of
8 o'clock on a Saturday night

My beach blanket radio still hums on
after all these years

I can e-mail you pictures Mr. Bob
of tigers, Corvettes, little green Motherboards and
black leather party girls in the place of your choice
if you want
as long as
you want me
you want me
to be your interactive imagination

Smelling the Roses

There is no air in here because he took it
gave it that Lotus Potion Number Nine
he bought last week directly sent from France
smells like bugs flying in my nostrils

That Boston bluefish frying in the pan he sealed
with lemon juice and vinegar
reminds me of that stuff he sprays on furniture to
keep the dust away
makes me sneeze but I didn't mark the floor
he scrubbed so carefully with
Spic and Span, Pine Sol and ammonia
burn my lungs out

Yes, I sprayed the garbage can with Lysol

I must be living with the white tornado whirling around
sticking air freshener decals on the windows
hanging insect repellant strips off the barbecue

I cannot smell the roses anymore

Peanut Butter

Don't do that

Do what?

Shoot that peanut butter in your arm
is it smooth or crunchy?

Smooth
they didn't have the one with
the peanut on top and
I didn't want to use crunchy
seemed morbid somehow

Why can't you for once in your life
do something more common like shoot heroin?

It's not for sure the first time
besides I might like it

How dreadful

It is
anyway it would be the kicker

The kicker?

To find happiness and then to die
are you finished with your crusts?

Yes, but hurry

October

I sit on the river bank and watch him reach over, pick up a rock. The river, long and wide, is mirror flat. He pitches the rock, smacks the surface. The thin ice snaps, smaller pieces disappear.

Your conceptions have been destroyed, he says. I pull my jacket closer to me, feel the spit on my face sting me. I want him to hold my hand, red chapped skin rubbing red chapped skin. I want him to brush my cheek with wet lips.

It is up to you to put it back together, he says. You cannot change what you see, only what you want to do about it. You'll find no sympathy for what you're going through.

Still standing on the river bank, his raw hands pick up rocks and throw them.

I am cold. I want to sit here and freeze a little after the sun sets. I want him to talk to me.

You've always believed what people tell you, he says, always thought that approval brings freedom. It is the circle that keeps you. What you really want is the ability to walk away.

There is fire and coffee in the air, but I know that it is his.

Help yourself, he says, you don't have to pay me back.

This is a lie, as is most everything else I know. I walk towards the fire and drink his coffee. I tell myself that I will leave when I am warm. The river will freeze without me.

The biggest danger for you, he says, walking towards the fire, is bitterness. You still think that you'll be important when you're gone.

His face is bent towards the flames, but I can't see his eyes. I walked away for seven years, he says, picks up a rock and sets it in the middle.

It will crack, I say, and, with a stick, push the rock towards the edge.

He returns the rock to the centre. If you let it get just hot enough, you can wrap it in your jacket and it will keep you warm for awhile.

It's a long walk back, I say.

He looks me in the eye for the first time, and smiles.

Raven

Raven had a craving for consumption of the kind that
devours souls
he understood monsters and the love of horror movies and
wanted to be beautiful like a damsel in distress but
Raven thought his body parts were not the kind a hero would
want to save not the kind of picture anyone would put in a
newspaper but more the invisible kind that doesn't take a
picture well or represent a cause that
could speak to the masses
his demise he knew would be unspoken and so he fought it
even though he wanted to scream

Raven wondered why he felt so dead inside yet
could destroy so much outside why
his mother always talked of what it means to eat well when
what she saw when she looked at him was the cesspool of
all her wrongs or so she said and
he wondered if others saw that too
what it means to have value that
doesn't come from a mother's love

Sometimes I miss Raven
sometimes I want to cry
sometimes I want to screech down like a soaring hawk and
eat his head

Raven laughed when I told him that
he scared me in a way that doesn't conjure up monsters in
nightmares but the other kind and
Raven understood that when I followed him into the
caves where the music flows into itself and
into the tunnel that connects us

We played a symphony that
made us both happy in the distortion and the
understanding that we didn't understand anything except
the disconnectedness of it all
the beauty in E major and F minor and I heard
hippopotamuses and dogs
cats and spiders
mushrooms and asparagus
Raven and me in a soup of madness and
I wanted to embrace it all I guess
with my arms my legs
kiss it control it but
it wasn't the kind of thing I could do that with and I felt so
inadequate so
far away so
removed

Raven met me in the caves several times after that and
other places too
he would show up unexpectedly
hug me, whisper in my ear, Hawk
I thought you were the hawk but I knew
that he was not the mouse

I learned to
not fly on Raven's wing in public places
sometimes inappropriately but it was all I could do at the time
I knew that he could eat me when he was peering in a window
or anywhere
a reflection on a car
a reverberation of words
a mouth a beak
wide and black like oil spreading
impregnating everything beyond anything that
surgery could repair...

People often ask me what I think about when I drift off
I want to say
I think about eating Raven's head but I
know that I am part of it all that
I want so desperately to consume and I wish that
I was outside of it all and inside
a time capsule when the door will open on an earth mountain
from years before where I can feel the blue of blue
a bird in flight
the redness of lips kissing
in the absence of anything except the
wetness of it all that goes beyond the possibility of the
ramifications that it's all an illusion and that
the only answer is that it is what it is because
it is what it is that I want
which is different
from an addiction different
from a compulsion different
from an obsession or a fabrication of the mind

But I don't say that when people ask
I say something about how much I like sunsets
the kind that fall without creating shadows

Sometimes I miss Raven
sometimes I want to cry
sometimes I want to screech down like a soaring hawk and
eat his head

Sometimes I miss Raven
sometimes I want to cry
sometimes I can still hear him laughing louder than a scream

Something Shorter than Godzilla

I can feel it like the waves crashing down on California but
the stars are gone and it's just my cat scratching my back
I wish my life wasn't so pathetic but I know
there are no surf boards here and the life boat's out there
saving someone else

Echoes, echoes are good for making sounds of life
I'd like to think that human beings are doing something good
when all I hear is cats and helicopters
when they've got their prey in their claws

No one told me I would feel like the next meal even
when I asked for the real story but
now I wonder if they didn't know how to tell me 'cause
it's them too who are feeling it
yet I see myself when I am 80
walking up a hill with a basket of blueberries and
children tagging behind me full of song

Childhood seems a distant eyepiece to me now
when I felt like something shorter than Godzilla and
maybe not so dumb or mean but big enough and
smart enough to know the difference and to recognize
my goals in life were never really thought as being worthy and
I guess that I equated that with me

It took me years to make amends with that
I'm tired of hearing all the bad we do to others when
the goodness in our souls is treated like a non-event but
I'm no better nor no worse when it comes to
gleaning facts from tragedy and
sitting in my easy chair whispering quite softly, oh, my my

It's something that I'd like to change as
change is something I respond to yet
not as much as I think I do or think I should or
so I've been told and maybe I am just a
happy hypocrite thinking how much better life would be
if only things were different

Acknowledgements

Many thanks for the encouragement and support to the publications who have published some of my work:

"B" after "C"; The Canadian Journal of Contemporary Literary Stuff; Carnival: a Scream in High Park reader; Common Ground; Illustrated Men Newsletter; Instant Anthology; I Really Really Really Hate Literature; The Mattawa Chronicle; Oversion; Plus Zero; Queen Street Quarterly; Sin over Tan; Toronto Life; Writ; and Writer's Block Magazine

Being a performance artist at heart, I would also like to thank the many venues, their respective owners and organizers who have given me the opportunity to feel totally alive on stage and to hear the heartfelt sound of laughter even in dire times:

Aladdin's Bookstore; The Art Bar at The Library, Imperial Pub and its earlier stops; The Bamboo; Beaches Bookstore; The Black Rooster; Café May; Dark City; Dundas Street Reading Series at The Library, Imperial Pub; Free Times Cafe; The Friendly Spike Theatre Band; The Horseshoe; The Idler; Late Night after From the Ground Up, National Festival of Canadian Theatre; Lollapalooza; Pape Library; Parliament Street Library; Poetry Express; Poetry by Candlelight II; Poetry Sweatshop at The Rivoli; Queen Street East Reading Series at Stratengers; Scream in High Park; and Sneaky Dee's.

Thank You
To everyone who has helped, encouraged and inspired me
to write, especially...

To the members of watershedBooks—
Lucy Brennan, Allan Briesmaster, Mary Ellen Csamer,
Colleen Flood, Albert Fuller, Maureen Harris, Merike Lugus,
Pat Jasper, Pierre L'Abbé
, Steve McCabe, Al Moritz,
Chris Pannell, Giovanna Riccio, and Linda Waybrant...

To Carol Malyon, for your support in general and editorial direction on The Eel Ladder in particular, and to Beth Learn for your guidance and encouragement on design and photos...

To Kathleen Aldridge, Anton, Phlip Arima, John Barlow, Jill Battson, Richard Bieman, Christian Bök, Dave Bullis & family, Brian Burch, Natalee Caple, The Colonnade Entertainment Business Group, Bart Cross, Don Cullen, Nancy Dembowski, David Donnell, Shaun Donnelly, Paul Dutton, Tamara Fairchild, Waheeda Harris, Fred Hill, Leonard Gasparini, Roger Greenwald, Richard Harrison, Ellen Henderson, Tony Hightower, Ellen Hitchcock, Michael Holmes, Peter Hoult, Stephen Humphrey, Ken Innes, Gayle Irwin, the ISPI crew, Gaye Jackson, Robert Jason, Clifton Joseph, Adeena Karasick, Anita Keller, Bill Kennedy, Susan Kennedy, Lynn Kinney, Bob Kirk, Rosemary Laberge, James LaTrobe, Richard Lawton, Gertrude Lavoie, Brad Luft, Judith MacDonald, Kim Maltman, Mac McArthur, Geordie McDonald, Keith McKay, Louise McKinney, Rob McLennan, Angela Mckenzie, Doug McMahon, Dave McManus, Peter McPhee, Jay Millar, Kat Mullaly, Mike O'Connor, Stephani Ortenzi, Brian Panhuyzen, Isabel Pedersen, Steven Pender, the Poetry Sweatshop folks, Dave Porter, Patrick Rawley, Matthew Remski, Margaret Riggin, Stan Rogal, Stuart Ross, Shelagh Rowan-Legg, the Rudden family, Ruth Ruth, Chris Sequin, The Silk Underwear Group, Carolyn Smart, T. Swift, Donna Kempson Szlater & family, Anne Tait, Dr. Ron Taylor, Ralph & Marilyn Tibbles, my trivia buddies, Terry Tompkins, Darren Wershler-Henry, Cliff Whiten, Paul Williams, Brian Wilson and Olive Wilson...

To Laurie Anderson, Margaret Atwood, The B-52's, Bob Dylan, Aretha Franklin, Marvin Gaye, Joni Mitchell, Edgar Allan Poe, The Rolling Stones, Twisted Sister, and all creators of sci-fi anything for getting your stuff out there...

To Mom & Dad for everything...

I love you.

About the Author

Nancy Jane Bullis lives in Toronto with her cat Henry. Nancy hopes to live on a boat someday. Henry is not so sure that this is such a great idea.